container
water gardens

container water gardens

Philip Swindells

First edition for the United States and Canada published in
2001 by Barron's Educational Series, Inc.
First published in 2001 by Interpet Publishing.
© Copyright 2001 by Interpet Publishing.

All inquiries should be addressed to:
Barron's Educational Series, Inc.
250 Wireless Boulevard
Hauppauge, New York 11788
http://www.barronseduc.com

International Standard Book No. 0-7641-1842-0
Library of Congress Catalog Card No. 2001086372

THE AUTHOR
Philip Swindells is a water gardening specialist with long
experience in growing aquatic plants in many parts of the
world. He trained at the University of Cambridge Botanic
Garden and the famous aquatic nursery of Perrys of Enfield,
and ultimately became Curator of Harlow Carr Botanical
Gardens, Harrogate. The author of many publications on
water gardening, Philip was also formerly the editor of the
Water Garden Journal of the International Waterlily Society
who in 1994 inducted him into their Hall of Fame. He
was awarded a Mary Hellier Scholarship in 1990 by the
International Plant Propagator's Society for pioneering
work on the propagation of waterlilies.

Acknowledgments
The publishers would like to thank the following people
for their valuable help and advice during the preparation
of this book: Anthony Archer-Wills, Gail Paterson, and
Emma Spicer at New Barn Aquatic Nurseries, West
Chiltington; Gill Page at Murrells Nursery, Pulborough;
Austen Zingell at Old Barn Nurseries, Horsham; Graham
and Howard Healey at Four Seasons Bonsai Nursery, East
Peckham; Mike Yendell at Aristaquatics, Billingshurst;
Stuart Thraves at Blagdon's, Bridgwater; and Stephen
Markham for the loan of a wall fountain from his
collection at Leigh in Surrey.

Printed in China
9 8 7 6 5 4 3 2

contents

introduction 6

tubs and barrels 8

oriental style and bamboo spouts 10

sinks and troughs 12

millstones and bubblers 14

terracotta and glazed pots 16

sunken containers 18

creative containers 20

wooden features 22

pot fountains 24

spouts and cascades 26

planted tub with fountain 28

barrel and spout 30

japanese-themed container 32

bamboo spout 34

36 miniature trough for marginals

38 dressing a sink with hypertufa

40 setting up a millstone

42 bubbler in a glazed pot

44 miniature pot pool

46 sunken container

48 watering can fountain

50 timber-lined pool

52 bog garden window box

54 ali baba fountain

56 ram's head wall fountain

58 water staircase

60 plants for containers

62 looking after container features

64 index

introduction

Although water gardening is normally associated with a pond, in reality this is not a necessity because very stylish water features can be established in modest tubs, barrels, or pots. Some can be moving water features with fountains, cascades, and spillways while others are planted miniaturized replicas of the still garden pool. There are even pygmy varieties of plants to suit, from tiny waterlilies to dwarf reedmace.

Any container that holds water can be converted into a water feature, and as will be demonstrated, even those that have holes can be successfully adapted so that water can be contained. It may be a small pot or series of planters, or a window box, elderly watering can, or wooden crate – with ingenuity each is a potential water feature.

Nowadays moving water can also be easily added. Submersible pumps are so compact, powerful, and easy to install that the smallest pot or tub can be converted into a bubbler or fountain. Modern pumps are very deceptive in their size and the relationship of this to output. All display the water displacement on their packaging, but for most gardeners the figures are meaningless when stated in gallons or liters per hour, so more visual means are required.

This involves careful consideration of the container and of the feature to be created, the flow of water being simulated with a hosepipe. Produce the flow desired by controlling the tap and then gather the water that runs

over or bubbles through the feature for a period of one minute. Measure the quantity collected, convert it into gallons or liters and multiply by 60. This gives the amount of water that a suitable pump must move in an hour.

Pumps are easy to install and are often attached to a ready-made container water garden. Barrels with replica hand pumps are usually available as a package. So too the sumps that enable bubbling Ali Baba jars and millstones to function so successfully. These merely require sinking into the ground, filling with water and dressing with cobbles to become functional. While it is simple to create a container water feature using prepared materials, a lot of the fun really comes from creating your own.

Plants are also important, as indeed are a few fish to keep down mosquito larvae, although the fish must generally be removed and released into a larger pool at the approach of winter. Plants are mostly hardy and can remain in a confined space all winter long, although pots and planters do provide a good opportunity for experimenting with a few sub-tropical aquatics, which can spend the summer outdoors in cold climates and be protected from the elements in the greenhouse during the winter.

Container water gardening offers great opportunities for imaginative planting and inspired water features. The magic of water gardening can quickly be yours to enjoy.

Above: The tropical lotus is often referred to as the seat of Buddha.
Right: A small mask spilling water into a cobble-dressed trough provides the pleasure of water without any of its hazards, and creates a cool, humid corner for the gardener to enjoy.

tubs and barrels

Of all the containers that can be used for creating a water garden, tubs and barrels are the easiest to assimilate into the garden scene. Mostly made of natural materials, they blend in well with traditional plantings and landscape features and give a rustic feel.

Originally the tubs and barrels that were used for decorative purposes in gardens were second-hand and had contained other products. Tubs were usually whole barrels which were cut through close to one of the central metal bands, thereby securing the timbers near the top. Often they were obtained in less than perfect condition, having contained tar, vegetable oil, or if you were fortunate, sherry. Such barrels not only needed thorough cleaning before they could be used as water features, but had to be kept constantly wet to overcome the prospect of timber shrinkage and subsequent leaking.

Below: A barrel can become an integral part of a garden arrangement where other pot- and container-grown plants are associated. Thus the character of the corner can be altered by the adjustment of peripheral planting.

Left: *A tub or barrel garden does not have to accommodate plants or always be of serious intent. The addition of humor to the garden is always welcome and is particularly useful in attracting young people to gardening.*

Above: *A water garden in miniature comprising almost all the components of a conventional pond, all living harmoniously within the confines of a tub. This is a perfect solution for a limited space.*

Manufacturing tubs and barrels for gardening is now an industry. They are constructed in such a way that they do not have to be kept constantly wet to ensure that they are watertight, and they are made from untreated timber. Often tubs and barrels that are sold at the garden center are already conveniently waterproofed inside so that only water plants and fish need to be added.

oriental style and bamboo spouts

The Far East has given us a host of ideas for innovative small water features. Their origins may be traced to functions as diverse as ceremonial washing or frightening away deer, but they were created in such a charming and elegant manner that when modern versions are introduced into the garden today, they are valued as purely decorative elements, their original functions being lost in time.

Much of the oriental style is dependent upon bamboo for creating the right ambience. Sometimes it is the great tubular stems of giant bamboo that function as pipes and spouts. This is awe-inspiring when you consider that these vast tubes are really the dried stems of a tropical grass. The

smaller-growing species produce fine canes in yellow, beige, or black and these are often turned into screening and matting and used for dressing wooden containers that are established as water features.

Bamboo used as a construction material in the garden offers great opportunities, for the Chinese and Japanese have created an enormous range of styles and patterns of arrangement of the canes that can all be adapted to western tastes. The association of both living bamboo plants and polished treated canes with water also adds much of the mystique of the orient to the water feature of choice and is easily managed.

Right: *This charming oriental water feature is simple to maintain and adds sound and moving water to a peaceful corner. The surrounding plants are naturally dry-land varieties and although sited in close proximity to the featured container, they grow outside the underground reservoir or sump area that services the moving water. A simple and effective arrangement.*

Left: *Part of the experience of a true oriental garden is the opportunity for washing. While the western gardener or garden visitor may not wish to take advantage of such facilities, they can serve another role, making an interesting decorative feature that requires little attention.*

Far left: *The various sizes of bamboo offer great opportunities for effective moving water elements. The visual contrast with the beautifully sculpted granite block and foliage plant has a pleasantly restful quality.*

sinks and troughs

There are many opportunities for creating interesting contained water features from sinks and troughs. Natural stone sinks and old stone cattle troughs are perfect – they use traditional materials that rest easily in the garden and are complementary to a wide array of plants. They can be transformed into miniature aquatic landscapes by the use of pygmy waterlilies and dwarf rushes, or else planted as a bog feature with plants that demand only wet soil.

Apart from stone sinks and troughs, man has manufactured a wide range of receptacles to fulfill their functional role. When discarded, these containers can almost always be turned into a water garden, whether

Below: A complete miniature water garden can be created in a traditional stone sink, although with such a small volume of water it is impossible to create a natural sustained ecological balance. The water must be periodically changed.

Above: *This sink contains plants that depend upon their foliage for interest. Only the iris produces colorful blossoms, although the sedges and rushes have interesting seedheads.*

white glazed sink or galvanized cattle trough. The opportunities for innovation are endless.

With the addition of hypertufa, a glazed sink can be turned into a replica stone one, and with brightly colored metallic paints a galvanized cattle trough can become a trendy psychedelic water feature. There are shiny metal sinks and stainless steel ones too, perfect for adaptation for the modern minimalist garden with its mirrors and colored glass chips.

millstones and bubblers

For the introduction into the garden of moving water that it is safe to have children around, millstones and bubblers are difficult to surpass. All the delights provided by the sight and sound of moving water can be enjoyed with none of the hazards. There is not even the labor of maintaining a conventional water garden where there are always concerns about algae, fish feeding, and submerged weed control. Periodically top up the sump with water to compensate for evaporation and flick the switch to activate the pump. That is all there is to it.

Construction can be cheap and easy or complicated and expensive – you have a choice. Kits of all kinds are available to enable you to do it yourself. The millstones may be of reconstituted stone or fiberglass and the cobbles selected and graded to artificial perfection with everything put together in a kit.

However, it is possible to seek out an old millstone and large stone trough or bowl, essentials of the 19th-century farm or mill. These are expensive, but really show their quality and are deserving of the finest reclaimed landscape materials to accompany them. They can be assembled as a do-it-yourself project, but are generally much better put together by a professional.

Below: *An unconventional use for a millstone producing a cascade-like effect. Millstone features are often more sedate.*

Above: *This millstone-like moving water feature demonstrates beautifully how water and stone can combine together to produce an aquatic "sculpture." The effect is so pleasing visually that no plants are required to dress the feature.*

Left: *A drilled stone provides a simple bubbling feature that brings the sound and magic of moving water to the garden, but none of the inherent dangers to children and little of the work demanded from the traditional water gardener. The attractive cobbles are grouped effectively around the bubbling stone but serve to disguise the reservoir beneath.*

terracotta and glazed pots

Terracotta and ceramic pots can make a most imaginative addition to the garden when used with water. Generally utilized for shrubs and border plants, with some adaptation they can be used to create a wide diversity of water features, not only planted arrangements, but imaginative displays with moving water as well.

Manufacturers have realized how wonderfully these pots and water complement one another and now regularly

Right: The glazed pot planted with a single dwarf waterlily forms a centerpiece and focal point for this sunken decked area. The circular walls, paths, and semi-circular backdrop echo the aquatic centerpiece. It is important with a feature such as this to maintain water clarity by regularly siphoning off and replacing some of the water. It is never practical to attempt to create a natural balance in such a small volume of water.

Left: With a little inventiveness, an interesting water feature can be created with a series of traditional clay plant pots inverted upon one another with a pump placed in a sump below, and the outlet pipe taken up the center.

make provisions for the inclusion of a pump or tubing in their designs as well as producing pots without drainage holes. In some cases the pots and accessories that are necessary to create a moving water feature are offered for sale as a kit with fitting instructions. These are a little limiting in their range and so the more individualistic gardener will want to select an original pot and make adaptations himself.

While these beautiful pots are excellent for moving water, they are also quite accommodating for planting. The best effects are created by individual plant types being grown in single pots and then grouped together in a pleasing fashion. Being mobile, they are very versatile. An early spring-flowering pot of marsh marigolds, for example, can be replaced with a summer one of iris when the marsh marigolds' foliage starts to look jaded.

sunken containers

There is a misconception that if you create a water feature in a container, it has to be situated above ground. Small volumes of water can be sunk into the ground. Indeed, there are positive practical advantages, for when below ground level there is little danger of the container being damaged by frost, and the wildlife inhabitants harmed by prolonged freezing. Perhaps surprisingly the winter temperature of a small volume of water in the ground is several degrees higher than that in a container above soil level.

Sinking a container hides it from view. The only practical concern is that the depth and volume of water are sufficient to permit you to create or grow whatever you fancy. Visually it is the surface area shape that is of concern. It matters little what the sunken container is made of, or whether it served a completely different purpose in a previous life. Thus old baths and cisterns are commonly pressed into use along with plastic storage boxes and trash cans.

The innovative gardener does not necessarily require a waterproof vessel – wire trays can be used in an excavation and then lined with ordinary pool liner. The effect is the same as that of a sunken container.

Right: This is a beautifully arranged water feature that demonstrates excellent proportions and conformity with its surroundings. Although the focal water body appears to be quite sophisticated, it is in reality a simple container sunk into the ground and dressed around with very large paddle stones. The strategically placed boulders and clever associated planting through the gravel create an air of quality and sophistication. Dressing the container with plants is unnecessary as the fountain draws the eye to the center and provides activity.

Left: Although this is clearly a container, it is sunk almost up to its rim and the peripheral planting extended to the edge to unite it with the surrounding garden. The cultural advantage of sinking a container is that during the summer the body of water is cool and in winter it is not so vulnerable to frost.

creative containers

The imaginative gardener or designer can use almost any object that will hold water, or through which water will pass, as a water feature. It may be a familiar object in the garden, such as a watering can or wheelbarrow, an old-fashioned radiator, or even a bidet. The opportunities for innovation are limitless.

Modern shiny objects fit in well with the trend for using steel and mirrors as well as the popular minimalist design approach. However, for more traditionally conceived

Above: Contemporary garden objects tend to contrast with natural rustic materials. The water containers must be kept clean for maximum effect.

Left: This model of a gunnera leaf is specially created for use as a small decorative water garden feature. Of natural form, it blends beautifully into the surrounding garden.

gardens, garage sales are a good starting place to search for suitable objects. Older style gardens, even those with clear-cut modern formal lines, don't mix well with 21st-century materials, but generally blend in well with traditional wood, slate, and fired clay objects, even when they are quite eccentric and have no direct connection with gardening.

Left: Natural materials like pebbles and slate can be arranged so that they appear as manufactured objects, but still retain their raw beauty.

Above: Gutter heads that are decorated ornately can be utilized in the same way as traditional wall masks and gargoyles.

Sometimes it is not a single object that provides the feature, but two or more that might be naturally associated with one another. This is particularly so where running water is involved and one object provides a flow of water into another. Of the smaller moving water features, the ones that utilize household or garden items are the greatest fun to create and stretch the imagination to its limits.

wooden features

Timber is not usually associated with water gardening, but if it is properly protected it is one of the finest natural materials to use in association with both still and moving water. There are few readily constructed wooden containers that can make comfortable homes for water features, but the window box is one that is often manufactured from wood and it can – with a little imagination – be turned into a great bog garden feature.

Window boxes usually have drainage holes and if they are constructed from wood require lining with pool liner for protection. Given that both water and saturated compost are very heavy, then the traditional method of attaching them by brackets beneath a window is rarely viable. Window-box features with either water or very wet compost usually rest on an outdoor window ledge, or alternatively are used in a different way in the garden.

Wooden containers or boxes that are properly lined with pool liner can make a great impression, especially when dressed with bamboo matting or log roll. They can be planted as a miniature pool or bog garden, as well as used to create a moving water feature. The opportunities for their imaginative use are almost limitless.

Right: *Wood is rarely associated with water, other than as a support for stream sides. It is assumed that water and wood generally do not associate well as the wood may rot. However, properly treated timber has a long life and when tastefully used, creates a harmonious and rustic association with water, especially when dressed with plants.*

Left: *This shallow water feature is constructed using log roll and a pool liner. While there is some feature planting, the main attraction is the heavily cobbled bottom, which is also mirrored in the pots. Although simple to construct, to work well it is essential to maintain high water clarity.*

Far left: *Log roll can be used in any configuration to create an interesting water feature. A small pool of this kind can be successfully used as a conclusion point or full stop when log roll serves as an extensive bed or border edging.*

pot fountains

Traditionally most of us regard fountains as jets of water that shoot into the air. This is almost a form of aquatic sculpture if you consider the different forms that the jets can create. Sometimes they emerge from an otherwise still water surface, although we are also quite used to seeing elaborate figures – be they human, animal, or mythical – spouting water from the most unlikely places.

It therefore comes as a refreshing change, when considering moving water for our smaller gardens, to discover that there are a whole range of free-standing fountains incorporated into Ali Baba pots, urns, and other containers that will fulfill our desire for moving water, but that can be placed on the smallest terrace or patio. They only need to be filled with water and plugged into the electricity supply to be fully operational.

Below: Traditional pots can make pleasing small formal arrangements. The water flows evenly over the pots and into the surrounding gravel, beneath which the sump and pump are located. The surrounding plants are growing in moist soil, but need not be bog garden subjects.

Above: *Although the chutes of water are important and create wonderful sound, they are mere acolytes to the central urn with its impressive bubbler. Separate pumps operate the urn and wall water feature, while the tasteful planting softens the scene.*

Left: *Pot fountains only work well when water clarity and pot cleanliness are treated as priority. For an even flow and distribution, it is essential that the rim of the pot is level.*

Pot fountains in their many colors and configurations are ideal for intimate parts of the garden that can be reached by an electricity supply. Placed beside a seat beneath a leafy bower, an urn gently spilling water over its rim into a cobbled base that is graced with ferns creates an ambience as close to heaven as we are likely to enjoy here on Earth.

spouts and cascades

There are many self-contained units available from the garden center that will create a fountain or spouting gargoyle in the most limited space. Some are so miniaturized and carefully contrived that they are merely hung on brackets on a wall where they create a moving aquatic picture. Such novelties are of limited appeal, but nevertheless they provide the opportunities for people with just a balcony or a tiny backyard to dip their toes into the wonders of water gardening.

Other than these, the possibilities for using fountains or other forms of moving water with containerized features are legion. Pump manufacturers have created tiny pumps that will move disproportionate amounts of water without being noticed. They are totally submersible, just placed into the water, plugged into the electrical supply, and

Below: Small-scale moving water comes in many guises, but few features are as charming as this bird-bath cascade.

switched on. Powerful for their size, they can be controlled by a simple regulator that permits a vigorous spout or a gentle trickle so that all tastes can be satisfied.

Moving water in containers is usually created as a fountain, for this fits in well visually and can easily be controlled. However, there are many opportunities for water to tumble and cascade on a small scale from one container to another, providing the inventive gardener with a great opportunity for innovation.

Left: *Discreet moving water can be as effective as a turbulent cascade, especially in the courtyard or small garden.*

Above: *In gardens where there is a contemporary feel to the design, glass or metal can be used to great effect.*

planted tub with fountain

The tub fountain is a very effective option for those who want a small moving water feature that is safe for children. It is also one of the easiest to create from standard materials purchased at a garden center.

There are a wide range of tubs available, some of the wooden ones having been used previously to contain other materials. These should be regarded with caution as the wood might be impregnated with pollutants, in which case internal lining with a piece of pool liner is essential. However, many garden centers now offer wooden tubs that are manufactured for the garden trade and often these have been waterproofed as well. Of course, there are also tubs made from other materials, and while plastics may not be the first choice in the garden, they should not be completely overlooked.

The selection of a suitable pump must be carefully addressed, for there should be over-capacity to give you the option of turning the flow down to what is required. Never select a pump that will just fulfill the task and no more. This is a false economy.

MAKING A TUB FOUNTAIN

1 *Select a clean, watertight tub. Be sure at the time of purchase that the outflow of the pump can be adjusted sufficiently to ensure that the flow of water provides the desired effect. Place the pump in the center of the tub and make any necessary height adjustments to the fountain head.*

2 *Choose suitable plants and place them in position. Some height adjustment using bricks under the pots may be necessary.*

Left: *An interesting association of fountain and crowded planting in a well presented tub.*

3 Place a metal grill insert over the pump and thread the plants through carefully. Make sure it is securely positioned, if necessary stapling it in place.

4 Fill the tub to the top with clean, fresh water. You must do this regularly to compensate for water loss through evaporation and splash.

5 Switch on the pump and make any necessary adjustments by regulating the flow adjuster control.

6 Once everything is functioning and the plant arrangement is satisfactory, carefully place saddle stones or cobbles over the mesh support to hide it from view in order to provide a suitable dressing for the planting.

···· PLANTING SUGGESTIONS ····

Plants Used
Iris laevigata 'Variegata'/summer/marginal
Lysimachia nummularia/summer/marginal/bog
Stipa tenuissima/summer/herbaceous

Alternative Plants
Butomus umbellatus/late summer/marginal
Cyperus longus/summer/marginal
Veronica beccabunga/summer/marginal

Right: The complete tub fountain is ideal for terrace or patio.

barrel and spout

There are a number of arrangements with barrels and replica hand pumps available from garden centers. These also have a submersible pump included and built into the structure. Unlike tub fountains, which require an outside sump through which to circulate water, the barrel and spout circulate between one another. Occasional splashes as well as evaporation cause some water loss, but this is not significant, although to retain the best visual effect it is wise to continually observe the water level and to top it up when necessary.

Visually a barrel and spout combination benefits from the addition of aquatic plants. They make little difference to the ecology of the water body, but frame the structure beautifully if well chosen. There are limits to what can be grown, because water can be quite turbulent and many aquatic plants, including waterlilies, would suffer.

Even the very resilient pondlilies or nuphars would not put up with the turbulence. Floating plants also suffer, so it is principally the more resilient marginals and selected submerged aquatics that can be used.

PLANTING A BARREL AND SPOUT

1 *Connect the submersible pump to the outflow pipe in the tub. This is sometimes already attached as an integral feature of the tub when purchased.*

3 *Position the plants in the tub. For most marginal aquatic plants, the depth of the water will be too great and so you must raise the containers on bricks. With tub culture it is necessary to confine the plants to small containers, so they will require repotting annually.*

Above: *Half barrels with hand pumps are very popular, self-contained moving water features. They offer an excellent opportunity for growing marginal plants.*

2 *Fill the tub with clean, fresh water. Switch on the submersible pump and make sure that the flow of water through the pump is satisfactory before adding any plants.*

4 *It is desirable to have a few submerged plants in the tub, but these will not make a major contribution to water clarity.*

5 *Although it is not essential to have fish, they are beneficial as they clear up mosquito larvae and other aquatic insect pests.*

····· **PLANTING SUGGESTIONS** ·····

Plants Used

Alisma plantago-aquatica/summer/marginal
Ceratophyllum demersum/submerged
Houttuynia cordata/summer/marginal/bog
Lythrum salicaria/summer/marginal/bog

Alternative Plants

Butomus umbellatus/late summer/marginal
Lagarosiphon major/summer/submerged
Myosotis scorpioides/summer/marginal/bog
Pontederia cordata/late summer/marginal

Left: *A version of the traditional barrel and spout with a swinging wooden pail.*

japanese-themed container

The Japanese garden is famous for its very meaningful, but minimalist design. Western cultures are fascinated by the sense of mystique that this conveys, but for the most part find the appearance of pure Japanese garden design and culture a little austere. So it is a popular practice to take a Japanese theme and oriental materials and to fashion them into a western creation that picks out some of the best, and often more colorful, aspects of our own garden culture.

There are a number of manufactured Japanese water garden containers and artifacts that can be established as miniature Japanese landscapes, but it is much more satisfying to create your own. With the ready availability of bamboo in all shapes and sizes from large tubes to bamboo matting and screening, it is not difficult to adapt and dress everyday containers and to transform them into something quite special.

With ingenuity, a Japanese-themed container can be transformed into a landscape that not only includes water as its focal point, but also draws on the tradition of bonsai, that is especially useful when gardening within the confines of a small yard or on a balcony.

MAKING A THEMED CONTAINER

1 *The wood composition box is treated with a preservative. It is especially important that the outer sides be thoroughly treated.*

2 *Insert a piece of pool liner. Make sure that the folds in the corners are strong and simple for ease of fastening.*

3 *Screw or nail wooden battens, beading, or carpet strip around the top to secure the liner.*

4 *Dress the outside of the box using fine bamboo matting. This can be purchased from most garden centers. It is cut to size and fastened in position with metal staples.*

5 *Fill the box with a suitable compost. When creating a bog garden, it is best to use a richly organic material. Peat-based potting composts are ideal if mixed with up to 20 percent by volume of garden soil.*

6 *Arrange the plants so that they have sufficient space to develop. Do not disturb the potballs unless they are very tightly knotted with roots. Always plant firmly.*

7 *This bonsai specimen adds great character to the scene, but it will not tolerate the wet. Ensure that a solid base is in position to keep the plant clear of the compost.*

Below: *A charming miniature bog arrangement with all the essential ingredients of an oriental garden in the style of the west.*

---- **PLANTING SUGGESTIONS** ----

Plants Used

Equisetum scirpoides/bog

Scirpus cernuus/summer/bog

Alternative Plants

Astilbe crispa 'Perkeo'/late summer/bog

Primula rosea/spring/bog

8 *Make sure that the bonsai specimen is level. Other ornamentation can then be placed artistically, taking into account the remaining space.*

bamboo spout

Although traditional Far Eastern bamboo spouts and deer scarers – hinged bamboo spouts that strike a stone when empty thereby creating a noise to scare away wild animals from crops – were often connected to large established water features, those of the present day that are used to adorn our gardens are generally container water features. With modern technology they are able to stand alone independently of a water garden. Indeed they are often most effective when established by themselves in dappled shade surrounded by lush ferns.

It is common to come across moving bamboo water spouts at the garden center sold as a package, complete with sump and reinforced netting cover, the submersible pump and cobbles included. Indeed, it is the submersible pump that has revolutionized this kind of feature for it is merely placed in the sump beneath the water that is circulated through the bamboo. Evaporation causes some loss of water, but for the most part it is very efficient and effective.

If you wish to be more innovative than the traditional deer scarer or *shishi odoshi,* then it is simple to create your own feature with water tumbling from one cane to the other, providing that the last drop to the cobbles on the ground is immediately over the sump that contains the submersible pump. Otherwise the opportunities for creating a contained bamboo water feature are only limited by the imagination.

Right: *It is possible to obtain a wide range of authentic Japanese artifacts to enhance an oriental water feature. This paving tile represents the season of autumn.*

MAKING A BAMBOO SPOUT

1 *The pump is positioned in the sump over which the stone bowl is to be placed. The internal load-bearing supports must be sufficiently strong.*

2 *Place the stone bowl in position so that water will flow from the area of the lip as desired. Tilt it slightly forward to assist this.*

3 *Place cobbles around the bowl to disguise the sump and to provide secure support for the bowl.*

4 *Position the supports. These are two bamboo canes of equal length bound together with twine or raffia to form a rest.*

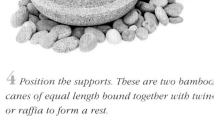

5 *Having positioned both supports, take the delivery cane and place it in position on the rests. The hose delivering the water runs up the cane at the back of the spout.*

Right: *Another option for a bamboo spout where space is very limited. This is based upon similar construction principles.*

⸺ PLANTING SUGGESTIONS ⸺

Plants Used

Dryopteris affinis/fern
Fargesia murieliae 'Novecento'/bamboo

Alternative Plants

Fargesia nitida/bamboo
Matteuccia struthiopteris/fern
Pleioblastus auricomus/bamboo
Pleioblastus fortunei/bamboo

6 *Secure the end of the bamboo water spout and insert the delivery hose of the pump. Test once again. Dress with rocks and plants.*

7 *The completed water spout is a charming and simple water feature with an oriental theme that can become an integral part of a garden landscape or rest easily alone. It is inexpensive and easy to construct and requires minimal maintenance.*

miniature trough for marginals

Ceramic bowls and troughs are very attractive possibilities for growing marginal aquatic plants, either individually or grouped together in an arrangement. There are also opportunities for grouping such containers together, especially those of varying shapes but the same general design, into more complex arrangements.

Most marginal plants will live happily in bowls and troughs, but marsh marigolds, irises, and the smaller rushes, such as *Juncus effusus* 'Spiralis', have the kind of root systems that will not overwhelm adjacent plants in a trough, nor become tiresome if confined to a bowl. They will require repotting annually, but will not normally out-grow their positions during a season and look tired and jaded as might more vigorous species such as *Typha angustifolia*.

When selecting a ceramic bowl, choose one with a good finish that is not going to fade or easily chip. Some are not fully frostproof outdoors during winter weather and if you select one that is questionable, then it must be placed indoors for the winter. Providing the compost does not dry out, the plants will come to no harm.

Below: Moving water is the principal attraction here. The planting, which stands all around the container, comprises visually appealing plants but ones that are not truly aquatic.

PLANTING A CERAMIC TROUGH

2 *Place the compost into the container. Use a proper soil-based aquatic planting medium. Where marginal and bog garden plants are being utilized, this should be about 6 in. (15 cm) deep.*

1 *Containers often have drainage holes that can be filled with a glass marble held in position by silicone sealant.*

3 *Remove the plants from their pots and plant them firmly. In such a small trough, they are planted directly into the compost.*

5 *The finished planting with water added. This is very shallow and will require regular topping up.*

4 *Carefully position the plants and add a layer of gravel to prevent the water from turning cloudy when it is added.*

PLANTING SUGGESTIONS

Plants Used

Houttuynia cordata/summer/marginal
Iris laevigata/summer/marginal
Zantedeschia aethiopica/summer/marginal

Alternative Plants

Iris versicolor 'Kermesina'/summer/marginal
Myosotis scorpioides/summer/marginal
Pontederia cordata/late summer/marginal

dressing a sink with hypertufa

Although it is most desirable to use a real stone sink or trough for growing aquatic plants, the reality is that they are quite scarce and also expensive to buy. With a little time and ingenuity, a traditional glazed sink can be used and converted into a replica stone vessel by the use of hypertufa. This is an artificial stone-like material that is based upon a naturally occurring stone called tufa. In reality it does not share the same constituents as tufa but, when well made, hypertufa can be close to indistinguishable to the naked eye.

Tufa is a porous rock, which in nature is found as a calcareous deposit on the bed of streams or in the vicinity of springs. It is formed underwater and when moved to the garden and dried off, it is used in the cultivation of difficult alpine plants. It is quite a scarce and expensive material, and the original production of hypertufa using sand, cement, and peat was intended to produce a cheaper alternative. Indeed it is used to produce tufa-like rocks, but also just as frequently to dress glazed sinks for alpine or miniature water gardening so that they appear as if made of natural stone.

PREPARING A HYPERTUFA SINK

1 Hypertufa is made from a mixture of sand, peat, cement, and water. The sand and cement are in equal parts by volume and the peat twice the quantity by volume.

2 An old glazed sink must have its surface roughened up with a cold chisel before an adhesive can be applied and the hypertufa mixture added.

3 Apply the hypertufa mixture with a small trowel. When mixing, periodically test the moisture content to ensure that it sticks. If too wet or too dry, it may slip off.

4 Cover the floor of the sink with well washed pea gravel. Not only does this disguise the bottom and the plughole, but it catches much of the fine waterborne natural debris.

5 To make sure that the water is absolutely clear and to prevent any disturbance of the gravel, pour the water onto a piece of polythene. This disperses the water evenly and smoothly.

6 *Position the plants carefully in their small containers. The plants should be repotted annually in aquatic planting compost.*

A water garden in miniature for terrace, patio, or balcony.

PLANTING SUGGESTIONS

Plants Used

Cyperus eragrostis/summer/marginal
Houttuynia cordata/summer/marginal
Nymphaea 'Pygmaea Rubra'/summer/waterlily

Alternative Plants

Juncus effusus 'Spiralis'/summer/marginal
Myosotis scorpioides/summer/marginal
Nymphaea 'Pygmaea Helvola'/summer/waterlily

Above: *Hypertufa provides an opportunity for the gardener who cannot afford a traditional stone trough or sink to dress his own. It looks good when planted with an arrangement of colorful aquatic plants.*

setting up a millstone

Millstones are wonderful for making safe moving water features. They were never intended for such indignities, but once positioned over a sump, surrounded by cobbles and tastefully planted, one could argue that they have achieved an even more elevated status than was originally envisioned for them.

Real millstones that have ground flour are not easy to come by, but today a wide array is commercially available in varying sizes comprising those made from reconstituted stone, concrete, as well as fiberglass. The reconstituted stone millstones are generally the more pleasing in appearance and once water has flowed over them for a month or two, they take on a weathered appearance and start to develop a green algal flush.

The most important visual aspect with a millstone feature is to ensure a sufficient flow of water to produce an even spread across a level stone. This may result from a gentle film produced by a strong silent flow, or a bubbling and tumbling from the center of the stone. Either way it is important that the pump selected for the feature be sufficiently powerful to deliver the quantity of water where it is required in an unfettered flow. The manner in which it appears from the center of the stone can be modified to suit your requirements providing that the amount of water being delivered by the pump is sufficient in the first place.

Right: *The bubbling millstone provides a most effective focal point in this very traditional garden setting.*

MAKING A MILLSTONE FEATURE

1 *Measure the sump accurately. By using two canes and a string, the dimensions can be transferred to the ground.*

2 *Remove the turf slightly more than the exact circumference of the sump and dig down to the required depth.*

3 *Level the sump and then secure and support it with pea gravel back-filled between the sump walls and the ground.*

4 *Position the pump in the center of the sump and arrange the cable so that it does not show, ideally by burying it.*

5 *Place the top on the sump and run the cable through the small hand hole that is let into the lid. Then adjust the pump so that the outlet is central with the hole so that the water will pass through the millstone accurately.*

6 *Position the millstone. That is achieved more easily with the use of two pieces of strong timber. It can be easily moved and slid into position when supported by these, reducing the risk of trapped fingers. Fill the sump with water.*

7 Once the millstone is in position and level, the area above the sump can be decoratively cobbled.

bubbler in a glazed pot

Not all water features demand plants or fish. Smaller ones are better without them, especially if the water is intended to flow. Such features are very versatile, not only being utilized as features in the garden, but also in the conservatory and occasionally the home as well.

The choice of pots is virtually infinite and most of them can be adapted to use as a fountain water feature. It is the selection of the correct pump that is vital. With most contained water features, the capacity of the pump should be larger than is required to move the volume of water intended, and this holds true for the smaller containers. However, it is conversely also important that the pump can either be turned down, or is sufficiently small that in a confined space it can produce the effect desired rather than dowsing the surrounding area with unwanted water. Today there are some very powerful miniaturized pumps available, so check their flow rates carefully.

Small water features of this nature are essentially for summer enjoyment outdoors; they can be utilized in the conservatory all the year around, but when used in the garden they must be taken indoors as autumn approaches and not set up again outside until late spring when the risk of frost has passed.

Below: *There are many options for displaying moving water in a ceramic pot. This one uses a specially made series of small saucer-like bowls on a central column.*

MAKING A POT BUBBLER

1 *The pump cable is taken through the drainage hole of the pot and the cavity sealed with waterproof adhesive. The pot is raised on feet to allow the wire to pass beneath.*

2 *The pump is placed in position in the center of the pot. Modern submersible pumps are ideal for restricted conditions and are easily adjusted to provide an accurate water flow. At this point, test the flow of the pump while it is still accessible.*

3 *Measure the depth of the pot so that an accurate assessment can be made of the dimensions required for the wire support.*

4 *Various supports can be used, but the most useful is a standard wire plant support for the herbaceous border with its legs reduced in length. These can be easily removed with wire cutters or bolt cutters.*

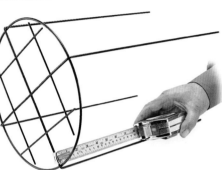

5 *The support is placed in the pot with the outfall of the pump emerging from the center. There should be sufficient room to the rim of the pot to allow for the cobbles.*

6 *A piece of fine plastic garden netting is cut to the shape of the bowl and rested over the support. This is intended to prevent any fine debris or stones from getting into the water. Dirty water is not only unpleasant but blocks the filter and sometimes the jet of the fountain as well.*

A simple but very classy contained water feature.

7 *Clean cobbles are placed evenly around the fountain jet. This disguises the netting and permits water to flow back for recirculating. The cobbles can be built up in the center so that the water emerges from their midst.*

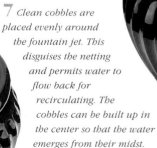

miniature pot pool

One of the most attractive contained water features is the miniature pool in a pot or bowl. This can be successfully established outside in the garden, although it is often thought to be more suited to the conservatory. For management purposes it is best left outdoors, because the water remains cooler and the plants grow more in character.

The establishment of such a feature is quite simple and there are some very interesting pygmy plants that can be grown in a confined space. It is good management that is vital if it is to be a success. There is nothing complicated about this; just remember that it is important to attend to the feature very regularly, almost daily if it is to remain in pristine condition. A few days of neglect and water quality will deteriorate. When this happens with such a small volume of water, it can have disastrous implications for both plants and fish.

Not that fish are essential, for the pot pool can exist perfectly well without, and with such a small amount of water there is little opportunity of striking a natural balance. However, a solitary goldfish can perform a valuable task in such a water feature, for it is the most efficient and biologically friendly way of controlling the mosquito larvae that will find their way into the water.

PLANTING A POT POOL

1 *The base of the pot can be covered with cobbles to the required depth. These will bring the small container-grown plants to the right level, 2–3 in. (5–8 cm) below the rim of the pot. The cobbles will also be effective in trapping debris, which can be periodically and easily siphoned out. The water in a pot pool will require regular replacement.*

2 *Position the plants carefully, making sure that they all stand securely. Choose plants that are happy in the same depth of water and with varying periods of interest.*

3 *Add water without disturbing the plants. Topping off with water because of evaporation will be a regular occurrence and periodic siphoning may be necessary if the water turns green.*

4 *The completed planting makes an attractive feature for terrace, patio, or balcony. A similar arrangement can be made for indoors if the plants are suitable.*

···· PLANTING SUGGESTIONS ····

Plants Used

Ceratophyllum demersum/submerged
Eriophorum angustifolium/summer/marginal
Iris laevigata/summer/marginal
Zantedeschia aethiopica 'Kiwi Blush'/
summer/marginal

Alternative Plants

Iris versicolor 'Kermesina'/summer/marginal
Myriophyllum spicatum/summer/marginal
Nymphaea 'Pygmaea Helvola'/
summer/waterlily
Pontederia cordata/late summer/marginal
Typha minima/summer/marginal

Left: *A pot of aquatic beauty. A single pygmy waterlily is growing freely in a decorative glazed pot.*

sunken container

Mention container water gardens and people tend to assume that the container will be sited above the ground. There is no reason why it should not be sunk into it. Sinking a container presents the opportunity of utilizing unsightly but functional containers that you would not normally consider. It also provides much easier opportunities for creating discrete and hidden reservoirs of water from which a pump can operate. Sinking the container also protects the inhabitants from harsh winter weather and in some circumstances permits fish to overwinter outdoors successfully.

When sinking a container it is important to ensure that it is well supported by the surrounding soil. Not all containers are of a conventional square or rounded shape; some are of a very irregular configuration. Apart from ensuring stability, it is also as important with a contained water garden to guarantee that it is level from side to side and end to end so that there is no undesirable overflow.

Sunken containers are rather like conventional pools and so all the precautions that are taken when creating a garden pool should be observed if success is to be assured. However, although many of the rules of the pool follow here, because the volume of water used is so small, there is no prospect of plants being arranged so that the water body can maintain a natural ecological balance. Evaporation and rapid temperature changes prevent this.

A SUNKEN CONTAINER POOL

1 *A simple storage container can be utilized to create a most effective pool when sunk into the ground.*

2 *Make sure that the container is level from side to side and end to end. Back-fill firmly and create a level area around.*

3 *Make a sand and cement mortar mix and trowel it around the top of the container to provide a bed for tiling edges.*

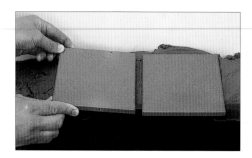

4 *Lay the tiles evenly around the container, making sure that there is a slight overhang that will disguise the edge. Ensure that they are completely level.*

5 *Place the plants into the pool before filling it with water. Only use dwarf varieties.*

···· PLANTING SUGGESTIONS ····

Plants Used

Eriophorum angustifolium/summer/marginal
Juncus ensifolius/summer/marginal
Mentha cervina alba/summer/marginal
Nymphaea 'Pygmaea Helvola'/summer/waterlily

Alternative Plants

Butomus umbellatus/late summer/marginal
Houttuynia cordata/summer/marginal
Myosotis scorpioides/summer/marginal
Typha minima/summer/marginal

6 *The completed pool will require regular maintenance as the volume of water is too small to sustain a natural balance.*

This sunken pool uses aquatic plants to create a balanced and harmonious feature. If you prefer a more lively effect, it is easy to position a small submersible pump to create a fountain or small water cascade.

Right: *Whatever your fancy, a small pool can be created with a container of any kind providing that it is liberally dressed with plants. There is no indication of the construction materials used in this simple but attractive feature.*

watering can fountain

Providing that a container holds water or there is a conduit for water to flow through an artifact, an opportunity exists for creating a contained water feature. Your main concern should be to check that it has not contained any pollutant and is made of a material that is unlikely to give rise to maintenance problems.

Wooden containers present the greatest hazard as they may have previously carried an oil- or tar-based product or been treated with a harmful wood preservative. Copper is unpleasant when fish are around; even short lengths of copper pipe being capable of producing toxicity that can

kill goldfish in a rapid and most unpleasant manner when water circulates continually around them.

Surprisingly lead produces no problems; neither does galvanized iron nor aluminium. Terracotta is fine, but check that it is frostproof. The same applies to glazed pots and bowls. Plastics and fiberglass present no difficulties, although aesthetically they are much less pleasing. Providing the vessels to be used are solid and watertight, and there is no danger of water pollution, then the scope for innovation is only limited by the creativity of your imagination.

MAKING A WATERING CAN FOUNTAIN

Discarded garden artifacts brought to life as a water feature.

1 *Arrange for a standpipe that is disconnected from a main water supply to be positioned as a water feature and use bricks or pavers to make a base through which a cable and outlet pipe can be fed.*

2 *Thread the pump cable through the pot along with the outlet pipe. Secure this with a waterproof adhesive and allow to dry. This provides the sump for the feature.*

3 *Position the pot so that the cable and outlet pipe can be passed beneath or between the pavers without pinching it. Make a simple connection to the base of the standpipe using standard connectors.*

4 *Place the circular support wires on the top of the pot or just within the rim. It may be necessary to trim them to size with wire cutters if the pot is not of a standard size. Specially manufactured supports for container features are also available.*

5 *Place the bucket in position under the spout of the watering can. Run a test to make sure that the bucket catches the water and that it flows evenly over the rim. Adjust the level beneath the bucket as necessary.*

Above: *This tilting water carrier has been given new life by conversion into a self-contained cascade. The grating covering the sump was retrieved from a greenhouse.*

6 *Dress the surface of the support wire with paddle stones. These are very attractive and easier to arrange than cobbles on such a restricted space.*

timber-lined pool

Timber containers are greatly underutilized as far as water gardening is concerned. This is a great shame as timber is a very versatile material that can be used to construct any plain-sided shape imaginable. It then merely requires lining with pool liner in order to make it watertight and serviceable. There are many different methods of applying decoration to the outside and a multitude of types of cladding material that can be used, although most gardeners will agree that the rustic look is generally most appealing.

Timber containers are normally easily moveable, which is a virtue when cleaning out is required, and they are usually visually amenable to being grouped with other containers. In some cases wooden structures can be placed together and then united to form a larger and more complex unit where water circulates from one to the other. Providing the pool liner is installed properly, timber containers probably offer greater opportunities for innovation than any other container or groups of containers.

Containers of timber construction look a little stark unplanted. As they are lined, there is always the prospect of the liner being visible, although if properly installed this is not a serious problem. Any lined water feature is better for being dressed with attractive aquatic plants.

MAKING A WOODEN POOL

1 *The lined wooden container pictured on page 33 is here given a makeover by the addition of tongue-and-groove wooden facing.*

2 *The outside of the container is painted with a suitable weatherproof paint. Two or three coats may be required to provide a quality effect.*

3 *Fill the container with water and prepare for the introduction of a pump to create a moving water feature. Do not fill beyond the top of the liner level.*

4 *Select a piece of dried tree root as the main focal point for the moving water. Secure the pump hose in position with waterproof silicone sealant.*

5 *The other end of the clear hose should be attached securely to a small submersible pump that will sit in the container. All joints and connections must be watertight.*

6 *Place the pump into the water so that the outflow pipe is disguised. Test and adjust the pump to ensure that the flow of water is adequate.*

7 *Add the plants and, where necessary, adjust their level with stones or a brick. Only marginals and floating aquatics are suitable for this feature.*

Above: *This pool conveys both a modern and rustic feel. The straight lines and the timber border set off the water perfectly.*

⸻ PLANTING SUGGESTIONS

Plants Used

Canna glauca hybrid/summer/marginal
Iris laevigata/summer/marginal
Pontederia cordata/summer/marginal
Stratiotes aloides/summer/floating

Alternative Plants

Caltha palustris/spring/marginal
Hydrocharis morsus-ranae/summer/floating
Iris laevigata 'Variegata'/summer/marginal
Zantedeschia aethiopica/summer/marginal

bog garden window box

In recent years there has been an explosion in the popularity of window boxes and planters for the decorative garden. Window boxes, traditionally functional and dull, and the preserve of geraniums, salvias, and lobelia, have suddenly been seen in a different light. They are not now always attached to window ledges, but find themselves in all manner of situations sporting not the usual geraniums or marigolds, but osteospermums, dwarf conifers, or maybe herbs as well. The staid image of the window box has gone and been replaced by a much trendier look.

Given the wide variety of window boxes available, there are many opportunities for utilizing them for contained water features. Truly aquatic plants demand a deeper box than the average that is available from the garden center. Also if you were to grow true aquatic plants, the weight of water would be such that a water-garden window box would only be safe placed on the ground.

Creating a bog garden feature in a window box is a completely different proposition. There is no requirement for standing water and the compost can be of a much lighter organic material than would be desirable for marginal aquatic plant cultivation. The rich diversity of bog garden subjects available also makes such a proposition very attractive.

A BOG GARDEN TROUGH

1 *The trough should be lined with black polyethylene to waterproof it. Add about 2 in. (5 cm) of a good aquatic planting compost. This helps to hold the liner in position and tightens it up prior to trimming and fastening.*

Left: *A series of wooden troughs with moving water that provide a happy home for variegated irises and arum lilies. The plants around are growing in bog conditions.*

4 *Set the plants firmly in the compost. Add further aquatic planting compost to top off as necessary.*

2 Trim the edge of the liner so that it can be folded over and fastened just beneath the edge of the box. Leave a slight excess to compensate for irregularities.

3 Fold the liner over neatly and staple it to the inside of the walls of the container with a staple gun. Only secure the top 1–1½ in. (3 or 4 cm) of the liner. Stapling lower will make small punctures and water may seep behind, causing discoloring of the wood and eventually rotting.

5 Upright plants look good with others trailing in the foreground. Creeping Jenny is the perfect foil for hostas and astilbes.

PLANTING SUGGESTIONS

Plants Used

Astilbe glaberrima/summer/bog

Hosta fortunei/summer/bog

Iris forrestii/summer/bog

Lobelia fulgens/summer/bog

Lysimachia nummularia/summer/
   marginal/bog

Stipa tenuissima/summer/herbaceous

Alternative Plants

Astilbe crispa 'Perkeo'/late summer/bog

Iris ensata/summer/bog

Lobelia vedrariensis/summer/bog

Lysimachia nummularia 'Aurea'/summer/bog

Primula denticulata/spring/bog

ali baba fountain

If you really want to be classy, then you can go for a mystical eastern look or a warm Mediterranean effect with an Ali Baba fountain. Tall jars and pots imported from abroad make wonderful features in a western garden. Not that they need be confined to a western style – on a modern patio or deck they can often be incorporated into the garden scene unconventionally, the overall picture being built around the featured pots.

When selecting a suitable pot for such a feature its outer appearance is vital. It must have strong color and presence, yet be able to accommodate the necessary tubing to permit the establishment of sufficient water flow to create the desired effect. There can be a considerable lift for a pump, depending upon where it is placed, and it is essential that the capacity together with the lift and flow required is carefully considered before the pump is purchased. An excess of capacity is recommended.

Ali Baba fountains are not year-round features in colder climates, because few of the large pots that are available to the home gardener are sufficiently frostproof to tolerate freezing when full of water without shaling, flaking, or fracturing. As winter approaches, drain off the water and seal the top to prevent snow and rain from entering. Otherwise, take it indoors for protection.

Right: While most Ali Baba fountains use the container to make a statement, this sunken version depends on two strong jets of water over layers of glass and pebbles.

MAKING AN ALI BABA FOUNTAIN

1 As the central flow of water must be accurately controlled, the pump outlet must be secured to a fixed copper pipe.

2 The submersible pump is placed in the sump prior to the top being replaced and the jar positioned. The electrical cable is disguised as much as possible.

3 Bricks put into the base of the pot help hold the copper pipe in position. The pipe must be central in the jar so that the bubble of water appears in the middle.

4 *Feed the hose from the pump through the base of the jar and connect it to the copper pipe. Seal the hole in the jar with a waterproof sealer.*

5 *Finally position the jar, ensuring that the rim is level to ensure an even overflow. Dress around the base and disguise the sump with fine cobbles.*

A solitary jar softly weeping and sparkling in the summer sun. The lilies add fragrance.

ram's head wall fountain

Wall fountains have a great tradition and modern versions of the masks and gargoyles of the past are widely available from garden centers. They provide a very versatile method of introducing moving water into the smaller garden without diminishing its importance. Apart from masks and gargoyles, there are also many types of wall fountains that are completely self-contained and flow into a raised or sunken basal pool, a bowl, or dish.

Wall masks and gargoyles are available in all sorts of styles and in materials ranging from reconstituted stone and lead to terracotta, fiberglass and plastic. Their appearance is obviously important, but so is that of the container into which the water is to spout. This must be of a size and capacity that will accommodate the spray, but also be of a pleasing appearance and in visual conformity with its surroundings.

Consideration must also be given to the wall to which the fountain is attached. Old solid walls create difficulty with disguising the discharge pipe from the pump and chasing a groove into the wall is often the only option. Unless carefully undertaken, this can look ugly. The ideal is to attach the fountain to a cavity wall and take the pipe up through the cavity where it will be out of sight. When all else fails, use an attractive pipe as a virtue.

HANGING A WALL FOUNTAIN

1 Masks and gargoyles are not the easiest features to fit successfully. It is as well to make all the connections in mock-up first before drilling the holes in the wall and committing to its fixing. Make sure that all the connections and the screw holes in the mask function before fitting begins.

2 Mark the positions precisely, holding the mask in position against the wall. Once the drilling points have been established, go ahead and drill the holes and insert suitable plugs. They expand as the screws are inserted and hold the mask to the wall.

3 Secure the mask firmly in place making certain that all the pipe work and connections on the other side of the wall are in the correct position.

PLANTING SUGGESTIONS

Plants Used

Canna glauca hybrid/summer/marginal
Cyperus eragrostis/summer/marginal
Iris laevigata 'Variegata'/summer/marginal

Alternative Plants

Ranunculus lingua 'Grandiflorus'/
  summer/marginal
Schoenoplectus tabernaemontani
  'Zebrinus'/summer/marginal

4 *There are usually covers or caps provided to disguise the screw heads and to conceal the method of fastening. Attach these and make sure that they are secure, sealing as necessary. The fountain is then ready for connection and use.*

5 *Connect the pump to the outlet and place it in position in the reservoir pool, disguising the outflow pipe at the same time. It is prudent to check water output at this time.*

6 *Add suitable plants. Take account of the water level and only introduce those that are compatible and provided one will not dominate the others. Select only those plants that do not object to constantly splashing water.*

***Right:** An attractive arrangement for a small garden with plenty of opportunities for enjoying plants, fish, and the magic of moving water.*

water staircase

The water staircase is a traditional way of moving water down a slope. In its original form it appeared literally as a staircase over which water flowed, the even spacing and rises of the stairs ensuring one of the most reliable methods of guaranteeing even water dispersal. Today it loosely embraces other acutely angled falls from one vessel to another in which the drops give the appearance of steps.

An alternative arrangement involves drainpipes that are inserted into a slope to create a step-like arrangement. This produces a similar effect to the traditional staircase, but as the pipes are rounded, the water jumps from one to another in a slightly livelier configuration and the water takes on a more silvery look.

Many water staircases are an integral part of a larger and more traditional garden pool arrangement, but with a little ingenuity they can be used in a more confined space without losing any of their charm, although slightly compromising their grandeur. Not that this need be a problem, for by adapting the original concept to something more modest, a smaller arrangement can achieve an alternative and more appropriate ambience for the modern garden.

A WATER STAIRCASE MADE FROM SINKS

1 *Cut a groove in the back of the lower sink to accommodate the outflow tube that takes the water from it to the upper one.*

2 *Make sure that the tube and pump connection will fit properly and that they can be disguised when the sinks are placed together.*

3 *The front of the hypertufa sink can be decorated with paddle stones. These are inserted directly into the wet hypertufa and then allowed to dry before the slate spillway is attached.*

4 *Cut a groove out of the hypertufa and the edge of the sink to accommodate the slate spillway. Use a liberal quantity of strong waterproof adhesive to secure it into position.*

Above: Water staircases can take different forms, from the traditional kinds that appear as stairs to other formal water drops like this. All work beautifully in the formal garden, but demand accurate construction.

5 *Place the slate spillway so that it overhangs the edge of the sink. The intention should be to establish an unimpeded curtain of water. The edge of the slate should be smooth and the slate level from end to end.*

6 *To disguise the outlet pipe of the pump, drill a hole in a similar-sized piece of slate and, using the same adhesive, stick it to the back of the upper sink so that the tube will discharge water unobtrusively into it.*

7 *Take another piece of slate the same size as the top spillway to create a fake spillway on the lower sink. This disguises the remainder of the pipe and serves as a visual complement to the other slate spillways.*

8 *Plants are added. Here a single plant is set in the water, but the feature is surrounded by plants to soften its outline. These do not detract from the beauty of moving water.*

Right: *Two connected sinks with overflows make a water staircase in miniature.*

--- **PLANTING SUGGESTIONS** ---

Plants Used
Cyperus involucratus 'Nanus'/summer/marginal

Alternative Plants
Butomus umbellatus/late summer/marginal
Typha minima/summer/marginal

plants for containers

When considering plants for container water features, it is necessary to understand their habits and behavior. There are five main groups that are used.

Deep-Water Aquatics

This includes waterlilies and pondlilies as well as water hawthorn and any other aquatic plants that root on the bottom of a pool or container and produce emergent leaves that float on the surface of the water. For the most part these are the pygmy varieties of waterlilies and pondlilies. Although there is an ideal depth at which these can be grown, it is often possible to flower them successfully in a container with much shallower water. They are quite versatile.

Marginal Aquatics

These are plants that naturally grow along streamsides and beside pools. They have their roots in water and in their natural habitat have to take periodic flooding. Therefore they are adaptable to a wide range of levels of water, although each has an ideal at which it grows best. Generally marginal aquatics will continue to prosper with a reduced level of water, but will struggle with prolonged flooding.

Submerged Aquatics

Popularly known as pond weeds, these generally uninspiring looking plants grow beneath the water, some occasionally thrusting up small flowers above the surface. In garden pools they are invaluable in creating and maintaining a natural balance in the water, but in the container water garden they are mainly present for the benefit of the fish.

Floating Aquatics

A small number of aquatic plants are free-floating. These just float around on the surface of the water and are generally very decorative. They are most unhappy in small containers where there is constantly moving water.

FISH AND SNAILS

A container water garden is not a suitable environment for fish keeping because space is limited, water temperature variation is too great, and in the winter the fish need to be removed to a larger pool in the garden or to that of a friendly neighbor and replaced the following spring. However, a solitary small goldfish, or even two, can make an important contribution to the welfare of the feature. Not only do goldfish control most pests of aquatic plants, but also the larvae of the troublesome mosquito.

Water snails are popular additions to the container water garden because they graze on the troublesome filamentous algae known as maiden's hair. This clings to the inside of the container and often invades the plants. Choose your snails wisely, for only the ramshorn snails with flat disc-like bodies are exclusively algae-eating; the pointed varieties such as the greater pond snail will eat algae, but only after they have chewed the leaves of succulent marginals.

Bog Garden Plants

Although tolerating periodic summer flooding, bog garden plants require constantly wet soil. There are some plants that are true bog garden subjects and others that are really herbaceous border plants but that will happily tolerate boggy conditions. With the contained bog garden, there are more opportunities for exploiting some of these border plants as soil moisture can be much more readily controlled.

Choosing Aquatic Plants

It is always preferable to choose aquatic plants from a specialty nursery or from a garden center with an aquatic plant department stocked by a specialist grower. Ideally marginals and waterlilies should be pot-grown, even if when planted in the container they are going into soil on the bottom. Never purchase aquatic plants that are floating loosely around in a sales tank. They will already have started to deteriorate. Bare-rooted aquatic plants are only satisfactory if received freshly lifted from the nursery.

Above: A small water feature that gives the gardener a great opportunity to grow and enjoy a rich diversity of plants.

Some garden centers and pet stores offer prepacked aquatics, particularly submerged and floating plants. If these are sealed in polythene and hung on a peg board, give them a wide berth. They heat up quickly and spoil.

This also happens sometimes with submerged aquatics that are stocked loose in bunches in a tank. To check whether submerged plants are likely to be a good buy, look at the lead weight around the base of the bunch of cuttings. Black marks on the stems in the vicinity of the foliage indicate that the plant has been bunched for at least a week and that the lead strip is probably causing the stems to rot at the point where they are held together. Such plants should be avoided.

looking after container features

Looking after container water features is very similar to managing a garden pool. The two main aspects that differ are the fact that most containers have to be moved indoors, or at the very least must be well protected for the winter in cold climates, and that however hard you try, it is not going to be possible to create a natural ecological balance in such a small volume of water. For this latter reason, and also from the point of view of successful plant growth, it is vital that the correct compost is chosen.

Aquatic Planting Composts

The compost that is used in pots or on the floor of the container for growing aquatic plants has a great influence upon their performance. It can also affect the clarity of the water. Healthy aquatic plants require a balance of nutrients in order to flourish, but these have to be available in such a form that the plants can readily assimilate them without any leaching into the water. When nutrients become freely available in the water, they can be readily used by submerged plants, and when in excess, by green water-discoloring algae, too.

Aquatic planting composts are the most expensive growing media, but they do have the advantage of being balanced for successful aquatic plant cultivation, the nutrients being available in a slow-release form that does not readily disperse into the water. Although good clean garden soil, especially if it is of a medium or heavy nature, can be converted into a suitable growing medium for aquatic plants, because only relatively small quantities are required for container water gardening, purchased compost is to be preferred.

Planting

It is important to provide sufficient compost to permit each rooting aquatic to sustain itself in good order throughout the season. In such a confined area repotting or replanting in the spring has to be an annual occurrence. The contained water garden offers conditions akin to that which the bonsai grower affords his charges, but unlike the bonsai specialist,

Left: A moving water feature of great simplicity and modern design, which makes a huge impact in the beautifully manicured lawn. Water is central to the feature and all its qualities are exploited – from movement and sound to sparkling and ever-changing light.

PUMP MAINTENANCE

Modern submersible pumps are self-contained and require little care beyond the occasional cleaning of the filter, although in a container water garden this requirement is minimal. Remove and clean the pump in the autumn and store it in a dry place for the winter. Replace it in the container or sump in the spring.

Above: *The component parts of a submersible pump showing several configurations of fountain and plain water outlets.*

capacity. It can be really debilitating for aquatic plants to be deprived of their full complement of water and then be subjected to heat from the sun. Most aquatics will tolerate warmth, but not "cooking" in the sun. With features incorporating a pump, it is important to ensure that there is always sufficient water to guarantee that it is submerged all the time that it is operating.

Tidying up any plants present is an ongoing requirement. Remove any leaves that fade and cut off dying blossoms. Keep an eye on submerged plants and if these start to become crowded, thin as necessary. Algae of the filamentous kinds, like flannelweed and blanketweed, should be removed by hand the moment it appears. If it is allowed to develop, it becomes tangled among the plants. Green water can be treated with an algaecide, although in containers where there is no sump attachment, it is easier to siphon off the water and replace it with fresh.

Overwintering

In cold climates it is important to drain containers and to remove all the water during winter. If this is not done, there is a risk that they will be damaged if the water freezes inside them. Some free-standing containers, especially those with aquatic plants, can be taken indoors into a frost-free place. If water is drained and wet compost remains in the container, marginal plants and pygmy waterlilies will pass through the winter successfully. Replant or repot in the spring and they will grow again strongly.

Submerged and floating plants are best kept in a light, cool, frost-free place until the spring. Place them in jars or a bowl of water with a layer of soil on the bottom and they will survive quite well. Many gardeners discard floating and submerged aquatics in the autumn and purchase fresh stock in the spring. When a goldfish is present, this should be removed to a good home, such as a neighbor's pond, and a new young fish purchased next spring.

the water gardener wants to achieve normal growth with restricted resources. Pots and aquatic planting containers can sometimes be used, but for the most part compost is spread on to the bottom of the container and the plants allowed to root into it freely.

Routine Maintenance

Little attention is required during the summer months to ensure the success of contained water features. Evaporation is a major consideration, together with water loss through splashes caused by fountains swaying in the wind. It is important to check daily to ensure that the container, and where appropriate the sump, are filled to

index

Note: *Italic numbers indicate references to picture captions*

algae 14, 60, 63
Ali Baba jars 6, 24
  fountains 54–55, *54, 55*
Alisma plantago-aquatica 31
Astilbe crispa 33, 53
Astilbe glaberrima 53

bamboo 10, *11*, 32, 35
  matting 22, 32, *32, 33*
  spouts 10, *11*, 34–35, *34, 35*
barrels 6, *8*, 8–9
  and spouts 30–31, *30, 31*
bog gardens 12, 22, *24, 32, 33*, 60
  window box 52–53, *52, 53*
bowls, ceramic 36, *37*
bubblers 14, *15*, *25*, 42–43, *42, 43*
Butomus umbellatus 29, 31, 47, 59

Caltha palustris 51
Canna glauca 51, 56
cascades 6, 26–27, *26, 27, 47*
Ceratophyllum demersum 31, 45
cobbles 6, 14, *15, 23, 34*, 40, *42*
compost 52, 62
crates 6, 7
Cyperus eragrostis 39, 56
Cyperus involucratus 'Nanus' 59
Cyperus longus 29

deep-water plants 60
deer scarers 34
Dryopteris affinis 35

Equisetum scirpoides 33
Eriophorum angustifolium 45, 47

Fargesia affinis 35
Fargesia nitida 35
fish 6, 9, 14, *31*, 40, 42, 57, 60, 63
floating plants *51*, 60, 61, 63
fountains 6, *19*, 24–25, *24, 25*, 26, 28–29, 47
  Ali Baba 54–55, *54, 55*
  ram's head wall 56–57
  watering can 48–49, *48, 49*

gargoyles *21*, 26, 56, *56*

Hosta fortunei 53
Houttuynia cordata 31, 37, 39, 47
Hydrocharis morsus-ranae 51
hypertufa 13, 38–39, *38, 39, 58*

Iris forrestii 53
Iris laevigata 29, 37, 45, 51, 56
Iris versicolor 37, 45

Japanese style 32–33, *32, 33*
Juncus effusus 36, 39
Juncus ensifolius 47

Lagarosiphon major 31
liners, pool 18, 22, *23*, 28, 50, *51*
Lobelia fulgens 53
log roll 22, *23*
Lysimachia nummularia 29, 53
Lythrum salicaria 31

Maintenance 63
marginal plants *30*, 36–37, *51*, 60, 63
Matteuccia struthiopteris 35
Mentha cervina alba 47
millstones 6, 14, *14, 15*, 40–41
mirrors 13, 20
Myosotis scorpioides 31, 37, 39, 47
Myriophyllum spicatum 45

Nymphaea 39, 45, 47

overwintering 6, 46, 54, 63

Pleioblastus auricomus 35
Pleioblastus fortunei 35
Pontederia cordata 31, 37, 45, 51
pools, timber lined 50–51, *50, 51*
pots 6, 16–17, *16–17*, 42–43, *42, 43*, 44–45, *44, 45*, 54–55, *54, 55*
Primula denticulata 53
Primula rosea 33
pumps 6, 14, 16, 24, 25, 26, 28, 28–29, 30, 34, 40, 46, 48, 54, 63

Ranunculus lingua 56

Schoenoplectus tabernaemontani 'Zebrinus' 56
Scirpus cernuus 33
sinks 12–13, *12, 13*, 38–39, *38, 39, 58–59*

slate *21*, 59
snails, water 60
spillways 6, *59*
spouts 26–27, 30–31, *30, 31*
  bamboo 10, *11*, 34–35, *34, 35*
Stipa tenuissima 29, 53
Stratiotes aloides 51
submerged plants *31*, 60, 61, 63
sumps 6
sunken containers 18–19, 46–47 *46, 47, 54*

troughs 7, 12–13, 14, 36, 38
tubs 6, 8–9, *9*
tub fountains 28–29, 30
Typha angustifolia 36
Typha minima 45, 47, 59

urns 24, 25, *25*

Veronica beccabunga 29

wall features *25*, 26
  masks *21*, 56, *56*
  ram's head fountain 56–57
water staircases 58–59, *58, 59*
watering cans 6, 20, 48–49, *48, 49*
waterlilies 6, 12, *16*, 30, 39, 45, 60, 63; *see also Nymphaea*
wheelbarrows 20
window boxes 6, 22, 52–53, *52*
wooden features 22–23, *22, 23*

Zantedeschia aethiopica 37, 45, 51

Picture Credits

Chilstone Garden Ornaments: 64 right. **Eric Crichton Photos:** 5, 10 right, 12, 15 upper, 19 (design: Sparsholt College, Chelsea Flower Show 1997), 21 left, 22 right, 24, 25 upper, 27 right, 31, 36, 39, 47, 51, 52, 58 (Marshalls Generation Garden, Hampton Court Flower Show 2000), 61 (design: Roger Platt), 62 (design: Alison Armour, Chelsea Flower Show 2000). **John Glover:** 1 (design: Chris Jacobsen), 3 (design: Robin Templar Williams, Chelsea Flower Show 2000), 9 right (design: Alan Titchmarsh), 15 lower, 16, 18 (design: Roger Platts, Chelsea Flower Show 1996), 20 left (design: Alan Titchmarsh), 22 left (design: Alan Titchmarsh), 26, 41 (design: Michael Miller, Chelsea Flower Show 1998), 42, 45. **Malcolm Little:** 21 right. **Peter McHoy:** 28. **Clive Nichols Garden Pictures:** 4 (Dales Stone Company, Chelsea Flower Show 1994), 7 (design: Anthony Noel), 8 (design: Andrew and Karla Newell), 9 left (design: Dennis Fairweather), 10 left (design: J. Dowle and K. Ninomiya, Chelsea Flower Show 1995), 11 (design: Suzanne Porter), 13 (design: Roger Platts, Chelsea Flower Show 1996), 14-15 (Daily Mirror Garden, Chelsea Flower Show 1994), 16-17 (design: Boardman Gelly & Co, Hampton Court Flower Show 2000), 17, 23 (Chelsea Flower Show 1998), 35. **Neil Sutherland:** 6, 20 right, 25 lower, 27 left, 49, 55.